MONARCH BUTTERFLY

Jolyon Goddard

Grolier
an imprint of

www.scholastic.com/librarypublishing

Published 2008 by Grolier
An imprint of Scholastic Library Publishing
Old Sherman Turnpike, Danbury,
Connecticut 06816

For The Brown Reference Group plc
Project Editor: Jolyon Goddard
Copy-editors: Lesley Ellis, Lisa Hughes,
    Wendy Horobin
Picture Researcher: Clare Newman
Designers: Jeni Child, Lynne Ross,
    Sarah Williams
Managing Editor: Bridget Giles

Volume ISBN-13: 978-0-7172-6240-3
Volume ISBN-10: 0-7172-6240-5

**Library of Congress
Cataloging-in-Publication Data**

Nature's children. Set 1.
    p. cm.
  Includes index.
  ISBN-13: 978-0-7172-8080-3
  ISBN-10: 0-7172-8080-2
  1. Animals--Encyclopedias, Juvenile.
  QL49.N38 2007
  590--dc22

                    2007018358

Printed and bound in China

PICTURE CREDITS

Front Cover: Shutterstock: Ronnie Howaer.

Back Cover: Nature PL: Hans Christoph,
Kim Taylor; NHPA: Rod Planck;
Shutterstock: John Czenke.

Corbis: Ralph A. Clevengar 33; **Nature PL**:
Kim Taylor 38; **Photolibrary.com**: Animals
Animals/Earth Science 10, Don Enger 26–27,
Todd Phillips 45, Donald Speckler 13;
Shutterstock: Aceshott 18, Joyce Boffert
5, Aran Brand 6, Daryl Faust 34, Ronnie
Howard 2–3, Cathleen Howland 4, 37, Cathy
Keifer 17, 41, Svetlana Larina 42, B. Speckart
14, Brad Thompson 9; **Still Pictures**:
Bios/Digoit Olivier 22, 29, Thomas D.
Mangelsen 46, Ed Reschke 21; **Superstock**:
Age Fotostock 30.

Contents

FACT FILE: Monarch Butterfly

Class	Insects (Insecta)
Order	Butterflies and moths (Lepidoptera)
Family	Milkweed butterflies (Danaidae)
Genus	*Danaus*
Species	*Danaus plexippus*
World distribution	Southern Canada to Central America; South America; Hawaii, Canary Islands, Australia, and New Zealand
Habitat	Gardens, meadows, fields, and marshes where milkweed grows
Distinctive physical characteristics	Caterpillar has white, yellow, and black stripes; butterfly has orange wings with black veins and a black border with white dots
Habits	Active at daytime: Many North American monarchs migrate south for winter
Diet	Monarch caterpillars eat milkweed; butterflies drink nectar

Introduction

The monarch butterfly got its name from the early British immigrants that first settled in North America. The vivid orange and black coloring of this butterfly's wings reminded them of the royal colors of King William III of England. "Monarch" is another word for a ruler, such as a king or queen.

Native American people also had a special link with the butterfly. Aztecs from Mexico believed that monarch butterflies were the souls of warriors who had fallen in battle. From caterpillar to butterfly, this fascinating creature is a wonder to discover.

Monarch butterflies are attracted to flowers rich in nectar.

A monarch with closed wings drinks from a butterfly bush blossom.

Butterfly Basics

Monarch butterflies are big butterflies. Their wingspan is 3.5 to 4 inches (9–10 cm). Like other butterflies, monarchs are active during the day. They rest at night.

Butterflies are closely related to moths. Moths tend to have less colorful wings. Unlike butterflies, moths are active at night. Butterflies and moths are insects. Bees, ants, beetles, and dragonflies are also insects. Like insects, monarchs have a head, **thorax**, or chest, and an **abdomen**. The head has large eyes and two jointed feelers, or **antennas**. Six jointed legs and two pairs of wings attach to the thorax.

A monarch's wings are orange with black veins. The wings have a black border speckled with white dots. The abdomen contains body organs. The monarch's head, thorax, and abdomen are covered in fine black hairs and tiny white spots.

Milkweed Butterfly

Monarch butterflies can only live where there are milkweed plants. That's because milkweeds are the only plants that monarch caterpillars eat. However, there are many different types of milkweeds—more than 100. They grow all over North and South America.

These plants contain a milky **sap** that is poisonous to most other animals. The poisons in the sap can damage the heart of many animals. The poisons are a defense—they protect the milkweeds from plant-eating animals. However, the poisons do not affect monarch caterpillars. In fact, the caterpillars store the poisons in their skin. That then makes the caterpillars poisonous, too, and therefore less likely to be eaten by **predators**.

Wherever you find milkweed in the wild, you'll probably find monarchs, too.

Female monarch butterflies glue their eggs to the underside of milkweed leaves.

Tiny Eggs

There are four stages in a monarch butterfly's life cycle. The first stage is the egg. When it is time for a female monarch to lay eggs, she looks for healthy young milkweed plants. A good supply of fresh green leaves will give her young plenty to eat when they **hatch**. She lays her eggs on the underside of milkweed leaves. A fast-drying glue made by the female is used to stick the eggs to the leaf. A female monarch butterfly lays about 400 eggs at a time.

The eggs are tiny—about the size of a pinhead. They are a creamy yellow color and have a ridged shell. This coloration matches the underside of the milkweed leaf. That helps keep the eggs safe from animals that might want to eat them.

Hatching Out

The second stage in the monarch's life cycle
is called a larva (grub). The larva of a butterfly
is called a caterpillar.

As the caterpillar develops inside the egg, it
changes color to gray. Just before hatching, the
knoblike black head of the caterpillar is visible
inside the egg. Eggs take about 3 to 12 days to
hatch. The warmer the weather, the sooner they
hatch. The new caterpillars are very small,
measuring about an eighth of an inch (2 mm)
long. And they are hungry!

Once out of the egg, the caterpillars eat
their own shell. After that, they begin eating
milkweed leaves—almost continuously. In its
first day of life, a monarch caterpillar eats its
own weight in milkweed. In two weeks, the
caterpillar will be about 2,700 times heavier than
it was when it hatched. That is if the caterpillar
has managed to avoid being eaten by the few
animals that are not affected by their poisons!

When monarch
caterpillars hatch,
their first meal
is their eggshell.

A monarch caterpillar begins to eat a milkweed leaf.

Munching Machine

Monarch caterpillars have distinctive black, yellow, and white stripes. The stripes warn predators that the caterpillars taste nasty. The caterpillar's body has 13 sections. It has three pairs of short legs toward the head end. The caterpillar also has five pairs of leglike structures called **claspers**. The legs and claspers help the caterpillar grip when it is eating or climbing.

A monarch caterpillar grows very fast. Its skin can stretch as the caterpillar gets bigger, but not very much. So the caterpillar sheds its skin, or **molts**, every few days so it can keep growing. A growing caterpillar molts four times. Like its eggshell, the caterpillar eats its old skins. After two weeks of munching milkweed, a monarch caterpillar might grow to 2.7 inches (7 cm) long.

Heads or Tails?

If you look at a monarch caterpillar, you will notice that both of its ends look similar. Which end is the head and which is the tail? Both ends have sensory feelers. If you look closely, though, the feelers at the head end are longer than those at the tail end. Another difference is that there is a pair of claspers at the tail end of the caterpillar. Whereas at the very front of the caterpillar there is a head with mouthparts and eyes. Monarch caterpillars have 12 eyes. Even with that many eyes, their eyesight is still poor. The feelers help them find their way around. They also swish away flies or bugs that bother the caterpillars.

A monarch
caterpillar grips
the edge of a leaf
with its claspers.

17

A growing caterpillar takes only 4 minutes to eat a whole milkweed leaf.

Poison Power

Although the bright stripes of the caterpillar warn predators to stay away, many animals still attack them. These predators are usually young and still learning about hunting. They have yet to learn to link the caterpillar's bright markings with a bad taste. A caterpillar has more chances of survival if a predator bites its tail and not its head or the rest of its body. When an attacker is near, the caterpillar wiggles its tail. In this way, the crafty caterpillar draws attention away from the rest of its body. As soon as the predator gets a taste of the poisons in the caterpillar, the enemy stops its attack.

At other times, a threatened caterpillar might pretend to be dead. It curls up and falls to the ground. When the threat passes, the caterpillar uncurls and climbs back up the milkweed plant. The caterpillar then gets back to what it does best—eating milkweed.

Hanging Around

After about two weeks, the caterpillar is fully grown and stops eating. It climbs down the milkweed plant and looks for somewhere to enter the third stage of its life—the **pupa**. That is the stage during which a caterpillar turns into an adult butterfly. The caterpillar might take up to two days to find a suitable place to pupate. Usually, this place is a leaf or twig high off the ground, away from hungry mice or other predators.

The caterpillar has silk glands in its mouth. It makes a pad of silk on the underside of the leaf or twig. The caterpillar then hooks its tail end into the silk pad. Its mouth lets go and the caterpillar hangs upside down. It curls the front of its body, making a "J" shape.

A monarch caterpillar
hangs from a leaf. It will
soon become a pupa.

A monarch caterpillar sheds its skin for the last time.

Caterpillar to Chrysalis

The upside-down caterpillar arches its back. That makes a split in its striped skin. The caterpillar then wriggles for several hours until it has molted for the fifth and final time. This time, however, the caterpillar does not eat its skin.

The caterpillar now resembles a large wet jade-green droplet. It is now a pupa. The pupa does not feed or move. In butterflies and moths, the pupa is commonly called a chrysalis (KRI-SUH-LUS).

Green House

The monarch chrysalis hangs still. The outer layer of the chrysalis dries and hardens into a green case covered with gold rings and dots. Inside this bejeweled jade-green case, an amazing change is taking place. The caterpillar is turning into its fourth and final life stage: the adult butterfly.

Scientists don't know exactly how this change happens. Substances in the caterpillar's body break down almost all the caterpillar's body into a green mushy liquid. This mushy liquid then grows to form the adult, or butterfly. The growing parts of the adult insect recycle, or reuse, nutrients from the broken-down body of the caterpillar.

Chrysalis Colors

After 10 to 12 days, the monarch chrysalis changes color. First it changes from jade green to teal blue. This color is a dark greenish blue. Finally the chrysalis case becomes see-through. The chrysalis now looks a lot like a shrink-wrapped butterfly. Its cramped and crumpled body with orange and black wings are visible inside the chrysalis. If the next day is sunny, the butterfly will emerge from its chrysalis. If the weather is cold or rainy, however, the monarch will delay its entrance into the world until the weather is favorable.

A monarch chrysalis hangs beside a recently emerged monarch butterfly.

Emerging Monarch

A new monarch butterfly is most likely to emerge on a bright, sunny morning. A crack appears in the base of the chrysalis case, near the butterfly's head. The crack gets larger and larger until the crumpled butterfly tumbles out of the see-through case.

The butterfly clings to the empty case with its two hind pairs of legs. Monarchs and their relatives are unusual—they do not ever use their first pair of legs. They keep these legs neatly folded against their body at all times.

A monarch butterfly
eases itself out of its
see-through chrysalis.

A newly emerged
monarch expands
its wings by
pumping body
fluids into them.

Expanding Wings

A newly emerged monarch has a swollen abdomen. The butterfly pumps fluid, or liquid, from the abdomen into the vessels that support the wings. That expands the wings. It takes about 20 minutes for the wings to reach their full size. Any excess fluid in the abdomen is passed out of the butterfly's body.

Butterflies do not eat. Instead, they drink **nectar**, a sweet liquid produced by some flowers. Butterflies suck up the nectar with their tubelike tongue. When the butterfly emerges, its tongue is in two halves. These two parts soon grow together to make a flexible, hollow tube much like a drinking straw.

Once its wings have hardened in the sun, the adult insect takes to the air for the first time. The monarch then begins its search for flowers with nectar.

Scaly Wings

A monarch's bright, orange, black, and white wings are covered in millions of tiny **scales**. These scales overlap, much like the scales covering a fish's body. Have you ever found a butterfly in your home and gently picked it up to take it outside? Did you notice a fine powdery dust on your fingers? Well, that dust was hundreds of wing scales. The scientific name for butterflies and moths is *lepidopterans* (LEH-PUH-DOP-TUR-UNS). This word comes from the Greek language for "scaled-wing." If a butterfly lost all its scales, its wings would be see-through, like the wings of bees and flies. Also the wings would no longer work.

A monarch's wings
are covered in tiny,
colored scales.

A monarch
butterfly has
big eyes and
long feelers.

Eyes and Feet

Just like you, a monarch butterfly needs to make sense of the world around it. The butterfly has two large eyes called **compound eyes** at the front of its head. Each eye is made up of about 6,000 tiny parts. Together, the eyes let the butterfly see almost all around itself without moving. That helps the butterfly dart away if threatened by a predator, such as a fast-flying bird.

Butterflies have very unusual feet—the insects can taste with them! When a monarch lands on a flower, its feet might be able to tell the insect whether there's some sweet nectar hidden in its depths. The highly sensitive feelers on the butterfly's head can smell and hear. They also help the butterfly find nectar-rich flowers.

Nourishing Nectar

Unlike monarch caterpillars, butterflies do not grow or molt. Their only purpose is to breed before they die. However, flying takes up most of their energy. Butterflies need a lot of food to fuel their flying. They get their energy from nectar. A monarch's long, hollow tongue is coiled up under its head when the butterfly is not feeding. When a butterfly finds a flower, it uncoils its tongue and sticks it into the center of the blossom. That's where the nectar is. The butterfly sucks up the sweet juice. Once it has taken all the flower's nectar, the butterfly flies off, with its tongue coiled up again.

A monarch uncoils its tongue and drinks nectar from a flower.

A monarch is
a skilled and
graceful flier.

Flitting Around

In the first three days of life as a butterfly, a monarch feeds on nectar. The butterfly's favorite flowers are milkweed blooms. But it also drinks nectar from red clover, lilac, goldenrod, and many other flowers. The butterfly flits around gardens and meadows, flying from flower to flower. Male and female butterflies pair up and **mate**. At night, the butterfly rests on trees or shrubs.

Monarch butterflies sometimes take to the air in clusters just before a thunderstorm. For that reason, the monarch is often called the storm butterfly.

Keep Away!

Like monarch caterpillars, the butterflies are poisonous, too. The adult insect still has the poisons in its body tissues that it had as a caterpillar. Birds that like to snack on flying insects soon realize that the monarch's bright colors are a warning. Most birds that eat a monarch soon throw up. After that, the birds avoid the brightly colored insects. However, some birds, such as orioles, jays, and flycatchers, can eat monarch butterflies without becoming sick.

Another American butterfly, the viceroy, looks a lot like a monarch. The only obvious difference is a black line across the hind, or back, wings of the viceroy. The monarch does not have this line. Zoologists, or scientists who study animals, used to think that the viceroy was not poisonous and had copied the monarch's colors to protect it. Predators would avoid the viceroy, thinking it tasted as horrible as the monarch. However, zoologists now know that the viceroy is even more poisonous than the monarch!

A viceroy butterfly hangs from a bunch of wild berries.

A monarch rests
on a tree in fall.
Soon the butterfly
will migrate south.

Fall Flight

When fall arrives and the days shorten, monarch butterflies stop mating and laying eggs. They drink a lot of nectar—so much that they build up a layer of fat. The monarchs then embark on an incredible journey. This seasonal journey is called a **migration**. The monarchs fly to their wintering grounds in the south. There, they escape frosty winter weather that would kill them.

Monarchs that live west of the Rocky Mountains head to wintering sites in coastal California. Monarchs that live east of the Rockies head to central Mexico. Some monarchs migrate only a few miles south. Others fly from as far away as Canada, covering a distance of 2,000 miles (3,200 km)! Not all monarchs make this long journey. Monarchs living on islands and in Central and South America have no reason to migrate. They live in regions where the weather is warm all year round.

Along the Way

When migrating, monarchs fly during the day. At night they find trees to rest in. These trees are called **roosts**. A roost might be covered with monarchs. The butterflies also stop flying if the weather is bad, such as heavy rain that would damage their fragile wings.

If the wind is with a migrating monarch, it can cover as much as 100 miles (160 km) in a day. The butterflies also need to stop about once a week or so to refuel on nectar. Monarch butterflies follow the same routes every year. That is amazing because no monarch ever makes the same southward journey twice—they do not live long enough to make a second trip. Perhaps they follow the Earth's magnetic fields or the position of the Sun like many migrating birds do. Scientists still do not understand how monarch butterflies visit the same wintering places year after year.

Male monarchs have a
black patch on an inner
vein of each hind wing.

Monarchs roost on a tree trunk.

Winter Roosts

Monarchs fly onto their wintering roosts one by one. The butterfly's favorite roosts are pine and eucalyptus trees. These trees are often so dense with butterflies that you cannot see the bark or branches—just a mass of orange and black wings. Some branches might even bend under the weight of the butterflies.

Pacific Grove in California is often called "Butterfly Town, USA" because millions of monarch butterflies spend the winter there. Breezes from the Pacific Ocean keep this coastal town free from frosts during winter. Each year in Pacific Grove, schoolchildren hold a parade to celebrate the return of the butterflies. It is even against the law to harm a monarch butterfly in Pacific Grove.

Throughout the winter, the butterflies stay on the roosts, occasionally feeding on nectar or dew. The weather is quite cool and the butterflies are sluggish. They are most active late in the morning.

North Again

In spring, the monarchs head back north. Many mate before flying away. The butterflies fly north until they find milkweed. The first stop for many monarchs that wintered in Mexico is southern Texas. Others leave Mexico and fly nonstop across the Gulf of Mexico.

Once the female butterflies find fresh milkweed, they lay eggs and die soon after. Within a few weeks these eggs will have hatched into caterpillars, pupated, and become butterflies themselves. This new generation of butterflies heads north, too. It may take three or four short-lived generations before the monarchs reach their summer homes. In fall, the monarch butterflies that emerged in late summer fly south to their wintering roosts. This generation survives the longest, up to 7 months.

Words to Know

Abdomen   The rear section of an insect's body.

Antennas   The pair of feelers on a butterfly's
head. A monarch caterpillar has
a pair of antennas at each end of
its body.

Chrysalis   *See* Pupa.

Claspers   The grasping leglike hooks that
a caterpillar uses to grip leaves.

Compound   Large eyes found on many insects.
eyes   Each eye is made up of many parts.

Hatch   To break out of an egg.

Mate   To come together to produce young.

Migration   Long journey made at regular times
of the year to find food, a place to
raise young, or warmer weather.

49

Molts	Sheds the skin all at once. Monarch caterpillars molt fives times.
Nectar	A sugary liquid made by flowers.
Predators	Animals that hunt other animals.
Pupa	The third stage of a butterfly's life cycle when the insect changes from a caterpillar into a butterfly. A butterfly pupa is also called a chrysalis.
Roosts	Trees on which hundreds or thousands of monarch butterflies rest when migrating or during winter.
Sap	The liquid inside a plant.
Scales	Tiny colored overlapping plates on the wings of butterflies.
Thorax	The middle section of an insect, between the head and the abdomen. The legs and wings are attached to the thorax.

Find Out More

Books

Cooper, J. *Monarch Butterfly*. Life Cycles. Vero Beach, Florida: Rourke Publishing, 2003.

Whalley, P. *Eyewitness: Butterfly and Moth*. Eyewitness Books. New York, New York: DK Publishing Inc., 2000.

Web sites

Monarch Butterfly
www.enchantedlearning.com/subjects/butterfly/species/Monarch.shtml
Lots of information about the monarch butterfly.

The Monarch Butterfly
www.kidzone.ws/animals/monarch_butterfly.htm
Photos and facts about monarch caterpillars and butterflies.

Index